the
SPEAKER'S
Quick Guide

TO TELLING BETTER STORIES

Connect with Any Audience
and Deliver a More Meaningful,
Memorable Message

DAVID P. OTEY

Text copyright © 2017 by David P. Otey
All rights reserved
Book design by Lancarello Enterprises (www.lancarelloenterprises.com)

Printed in the United States of America.

The World Championship of Public Speaking® is a registered trademark of Toastmasters International.

No part of this book may be reproduced, or stored in a retrieval system, or transmitted in any form or by any means, electronic, mechanical, photocopying, recording, or otherwise, without express written permission of the publisher. Please direct inquiries via mail to the publisher at the address below.

Published by Speaking of Solutions, LLC, P.O. Box 1322, Golden, CO 80402

ISBN-10: 0-9992744-0-6
ISBN-13: 978-0-9992744-0-8

To Susan, the most important person in my life.

CONTENTS

Preface *Page 7*

Chapter 1 | Why stories are your most powerful tool for swaying an audience *Page 11*

Chapter 2 | Know your objective: what a story should accomplish *Page 19*

Chapter 3 | Know your tools: what elements are needed *Page 33*

Chapter 4 | Assemble your winning story *Page 43*

Chapter 5 | You had to be there: how to tell it *Page 51*

Chapter 6 | How to maximize your impact with humor *Page 59*

Chapter 7 | Advanced techniques for storytelling power *Page 67*

Epilogue | Your story file *Page 75*

About the author *Page 77*

PREFACE

This book grew out of my experience as a speaker and speaking coach. But more than that, it grew out of my experience as a student of public speaking. It was only when I became seriously interested in improving my own speaking—interested enough to seek out the expertise of speakers I admired, to receive training and coaching from them, and to attend events where I could learn from them—that I began to see my problem. I didn't know what I didn't know. That is to say, there are the known unknowns—the questions you have asked that have not yet been answered—and the unknown unknowns—the answers to questions you don't even know to ask.

This point was driven home for me through my participation, starting in 2005, in an organization known as Toastmasters International. Toastmasters (more information at http://www.toastmasters.org/) is a U.S.-based organization dedicated to helping people develop their communication and leadership skills. One way it encourages the development of speaking skills is by sponsoring the annual International Speaking Competition, a six-round contest that proceeds from the local club level all the way to the World Championship of Public Speaking (WCPS). In 2009, I reached the fifth level of that competition. When I attended that fifth stage, at which I took third place, I had the pleasure of meeting Craig Valentine, who had won the WCPS ten years earlier.

It is no exaggeration to say that meeting and hearing Craig Valentine changed my life. I had just begun transitioning out of my previous career in broadcast engineering and pondering the advice of friends and colleagues who said I should consider a speaking career. When I heard Craig speak at that convention in Winnipeg on the topic of storytelling (of course, I considered myself a good storyteller, having won four stages of competition already) I was astounded. And humbled. Here was someone revealing to me just how much I did not yet know about the skill of storytelling, and doing it with a level of energy, humor, and vulnerability that made me say, "I want to do that!"

Since that time, I have met several other individuals who have claimed the title World Champion of Public Speaking. The ones who have influenced me most, besides Craig, are the ones whose training I have sought out, especially Ed Tate (2000) and Darren LaCroix (2001). Each has made a name for himself, not just by winning the title but also by his willingness to share what he learned along the way. And each has had an influence on this book.

What I have learned most from my study of world-class speaking is that it is not simply "a gift." Rather, it is a set of skills that can be learned and applied by anyone with a certain degree of self-awareness, a strong desire, and a willingness to be a student. If you have those traits, you, too, can become a more accomplished, more admired, and more confident public speaker. This book—and the forthcoming books in the *Speaker's Quick Guide* series—can help you acquire the skills you need.

This first volume of the *Speaker's Quick Guide* series is intended for beginning to emergent speakers. If you have been speaking professionally for years, chances are you have already been exposed to these ideas, although I like to think you may still benefit from my presentation of them. But if not—if you are new or just starting out, or if you are someone who has to speak from time to time in your professional life and you find the prospect daunting—then this is the book (and the series) for you. If I can make the transition from engineer to professional public speaker, you can learn to overcome your speaking challenges as well. And a good place to start is by learning to tell stories well and to use them to anchor the points in your speech. That is precisely what you will learn from this book.

Before you learn how to craft and deliver a story, you must know something about stories—about how they are powerful and why you want to use them. That is covered in Chapter One. Chapter Two goes into more detail about what a story should do for you as a speaker. The next two chapters are more nuts-and-bolts, going into what elements are needed and how to assemble them. Delivery is covered in Chapter Five. How (and even whether) to get laughs from your stories is the subject of Chapter Six. Finally, Chapter Seven introduces a couple of advanced techniques that will give your stories even more power. It is my sincere hope that these seven chapters will help you in your personal and professional development as you build your speaking skills.

Author's note: Some of the material in this book has previously appeared in my blog, "The Art and Science of Being Heard," which can be found at http://davidoteysos.com/blog. Portions of Chapter One previously appeared in Chapter 19 ("Upholding the Grand Bargain: Why You MUST Connect Emotionally with Your Audience"), which I contributed to *World Class Speaking in Action* (2015) by Craig Valentine and Mitch Meyerson.

CHAPTER 1

Why stories are your most powerful tool for swaying an audience

"Facts don't persuade, feelings do. And stories are the best way to get at those feelings."

TOM ASACKER

Throughout this book, you will pick up invaluable tools for making people *feel* something. You can use these tools to build a stronger audience connection than you may ever have thought possible. But the tools will be wasted if you are not motivated to use them. Therefore, this first chapter will focus on the *Why*. Why is it important for a speaker to be able to tell a story well? There are several reasons, which we'll explore together shortly. In sum, however, they all boil down to one word: connection.

You have to make a connection *with* your audience to make a difference *to* your audience. It's that simple. And if you're reading this book, then I assume you are out to make a difference to someone. By making a difference, I mean accomplishing your specific purpose as a speaker.

What is a specific purpose? To begin with, it is not a two-word phrase like "to educate" or "to inspire" or "to inform." Those are general purposes. Your specific purpose is the answer to this question: "What do I want my listeners to think, do, or feel differently when I am done?" Until you know the answer to that question, you are not ready to begin.

Note that your specific purpose is about *making a difference*. You are out to change your audience's condition by changing the way they think, act, or feel. But you cannot change the way they think or act without first changing the way they feel about you and your message. That's where the importance of connecting comes into play.

To make a difference, you have to be understood and remembered

Hall of Fame speaker Patricia Fripp says, "You can connect with your audience two ways: intellectually—with your message—or emotionally. You don't need to connect emotionally—unless you want your message to be remembered." And who doesn't want to be remembered? Fripp (as she prefers to be known) is exactly right when she says an emotional connection is required. Modern neuroscience has demonstrated that our decision-making center is deep in the emotional part of the brain. That means that every decision you make—including the decision you are making right now whether to believe what you are reading—is ultimately emotional. Every good salesman knows that a purchasing decision is made emotionally and justified with reason. As it turns out, that's just as true about whether your audience is buying the ideas you are "selling."

How do you persuade someone at an emotional level? Tell a story. Stories are the most fundamental unit of human interaction. In fact, recent scientific discoveries have shed light on just how stories influence us. Our response to a story arises from the action of a chemical in the brain called oxytocin. (Not to be confused with OxyContin, a highly addictive opioid drug.) Oxytocin is a neurotransmitter that motivates cooperation with, and empathy for, other people. You can trigger the brain's release of oxytocin by intimate physical contact or even by petting your dog. As it turns out, you can also trigger it by telling someone a story!

A Harvard researcher named Paul J. Zak has studied oxytocin. One of his findings is that character-driven stories cause oxytocin levels to rise. He also discovered that it is important for a story to depict a conflict or struggle. It has to do with getting and keeping the listener's attention. Here's how he put it in the *Harvard Business Review*:

> We discovered that...a story must first sustain attention—a scarce resource in the brain—by developing tension during the narrative...My experiments show that character-driven stories with

emotional content result in a better understanding of the key points a speaker wishes to make and enable better recall of these points weeks later.

Better understanding and better recall. As a speaker, isn't that what you want? The tool for doing that—according to experimental evidence—is a well-told story. That is, a story with clearly drawn characters and some kind of central conflict or tension. The more the tension, the greater the rise in oxytocin and the stronger our desire to empathize with the central character in the story.

When you tell a personal story properly—and tell it well, with some degree of conflict that escalates, and then is resolved—you get the audience to want what you want. If they see that your condition was changed as a result of what happened to you, they will want that change for themselves. And it's all because of the release of oxytocin. Storytelling, it turns out, is not just art—it's science!

You owe your audience an emotional experience

How much do you get paid to speak? Regardless of how you answered that question—or if you've never received money to speak—there is one form of payment every speaker wants. We want our listeners to *pay attention*. That simple fact brings us to a second reason for connecting emotionally. If you want audiences to pay attention, you must uphold your end of the Grand Bargain.

What is the Grand Bargain? It is the deal the speaker

makes in return for the audience's attention. I know what you are probably thinking: *audience members willingly give the speaker their attention in return for the information being delivered, right?* Not necessarily.

If you are just trading information for attention, your audience is getting a lousy deal. The average English speaker speaks at a rate of 125 to 150 words per minute. The average adult reading speed is twice that. That means if you were to write down your thirty-minute speech or sermon and hand it to me, I could probably read it in fifteen minutes or less.

But let's say you didn't write it down. Let us assume that you are delivering it live and I am in your audience. You are giving me what amounts to fifteen minutes' worth of information (using the written version as our yardstick) and taking thirty minutes of my time in return. If you want me to accept that deal, you must "bring something else to the table" as the saying goes. That is the Grand Bargain.

So what do you bring to the table? You bring everything an information-filled piece of paper lacks. You bring awareness that people connect with the spoken word at a different level than they do the written word. You bring the ability to draw your listeners into your stories so completely that they feel what your characters feel. When you do that, they will eagerly trade their attention, not for the information, but for the feelings you are giving them. If you want to get paid, you have to earn it. Even if all they are paying is attention. You owe them an experience they cannot get from the printed page: emotional engagement.

As Fripp says, "People will not remember your words, but

they will remember how they felt when they heard you say them."

Information doesn't sell itself

As you have seen, information alone is not enough to engage the listener and forge the emotional connection that will change the audience's condition. For that, you need stories. Stories, and the oxytocin that results from experiencing them, are how we forge bonds of empathy with each other.

But there is a chance you are still resisting that idea. I know this because I have seen it in my coaching. Clients say to me, "But, David, what if I don't have a story to tell? I've got compelling information, and I believe I can be persuasive without telling a story." Is this your sentiment as well?

Remember what I said about decision-making: it takes place in the emotional part of the brain. Before your information can make a difference to a listener, he or she has to make three key decisions: *Do I accept this information as true? Is it worth the effort to remember it? Am I going to act on it?* Those decisions will not go in your favor unless you make an emotional connection with the listener. Information alone does not do that; stories do.

Not only that, but you *do* have a story, whether you realize it or not. It's the story of how you became convinced that the information you have is important enough to share. The story is already there; it just needs to be uncovered. Think of the following questions as tools you can use to uncover the story behind your data:

- What did this information mean to you when you first learned it?
- What need drove you to discover this information?
- What makes it so compelling that it must be shared?
- How are you living differently now that you are aware of this information?
- How has it made a difference to someone else?
- What difference *might* it have made had it been known sooner?
- When have you seen your evidence in action?
- What have you seen happen in the life of another person that brings this concept to life?

If you will spend some time thinking about—or better yet, writing down—your answers to these questions, I'm confident that one or more of them will lead you to a story. And that story, once shaped and fleshed out, will lead to a deeper connection with your audience and a greater acceptance of your information. You will find the keys to shaping, fleshing out, and delivering that story in this book.

So far, we have seen that decision-making is ultimately emotional, and that a well-crafted story holds the key to making an emotional connection that will get your audience on your side. Only then can you influence them to think, feel, or act differently. In the next two chapters, the focus shifts from *Why* to *What*: what objectives you are trying to accomplish with your story, and what elements are required to make a story effective as a speaking tool. Subsequent chapters will shed light on the *How*. But never lose sight of why this is an effort worth making. As a speaker friend of mine said, "To change a mind, you have to touch a heart."

CHAPTER 2

Know your objective: what a story should accomplish

"The purpose of a storyteller is not to tell you how to think, but to give you questions to think upon."

BRANDON SANDERSON, *The Way of Kings*

The unfortunate fact is that many speakers are poor storytellers. There are many reasons for this. They may shy away from conflict, or weigh a story down with too much background. They may put so much detail in their stories that the listener's imagination is left with little to do. Or they may ruin a perfectly good story with poor delivery techniques. But often, speakers tell stories poorly because they simply don't know what they are trying to accomplish. That challenge lies at the heart of this chapter.

In Chapter One, you learned the reasons for using stories in your speaking, based on the overall goal of making a connection with the audience. In this chapter, you will discover three particular objectives you should consider when using stories, in order to accomplish your specific purpose of changing your listeners' thoughts, feelings, and actions. As we drill down on particular objectives, however, never lose sight of the most basic function of a story in your speech, which is to make an emotional connection with your audience. That connection—that boost in your oxytocin that comes from hearing a story—is what allows your points to be understood and remembered, and creates empathy for the story's central character. Empathy is what makes the listener want what the character wants. Always be clear on what the main character in the story wants. The pursuit of that desire should be closely linked to the point you are trying to make by telling the story.

Use your story to anchor a main point

This bring us to the first objective in telling a story: anchoring a point. An "anchor," to a speaker, is simply a rhetorical technique for making a point clear and memorable. An anchor may be an acronym (such as "FEAR stands for False Evidence Appearing Real"); it may be an analogy; it may even be an activity that gets people out of their seats for a few moments. But the most frequently used anchor is a story.

Here is where inexperienced speakers often make their first big mistake. They think of a story primarily as a way to amuse or entertain their audience. Unless you have been engaged as an entertainer, this is the wrong approach. Each story you select should have value in reinforcing a key point you are making. The oft-repeated advice for making a speech (generally attributed to Bill Gove) goes something like, "Tell a story; make a point. Tell another story; make another point. Tell another story; make another point."

This means that before you can select a story to tell, you must know what point(s) you are trying to make. This, in turn, means being clear on your specific purpose, as defined in Chapter One. Trying to build your speech around a favorite story, instead of starting with your specific purpose, is sure to send you down a rabbit hole. (Trust me—I've been there!)

That's not to say you won't prefer some stories over others based on their entertainment value. It's just that entertainment cannot be your sole criterion. Each story you select must relate to a point. Fortunately, you will often be able to think of more than one point you could illustrate with a given story.

For example, I tell an amusing story of when I was a twenty-year-old radio disc jockey pressed into service as a circus clown. I know I can get a laugh with it, because the climax is me falling flat on my face in the center ring of a circus! But what is the point?

To find the point of a story, look at who the central character is and what he or she most wants. (You will learn more about this story model in the next chapter.) When I approached the story as "I got to be a clown in a circus one day," there wasn't enough tension to make it a story worth telling. But when I realized that the central character was a shallow young man who wanted desperately to avoid public embarrassment, but who learned he could fall on his face and get back up again, the story took on a new significance. I could use it to illustrate any number of points relating to personal growth, such as…

- Falling is not failing.
- Falling forward is still progress.
- Growth opportunities come in many disguises.

…or even "Never trust anyone whose smile is painted on!"

But the point is, I had no business using that story until I knew I had a point to make, in support of a clearly stated purpose, for which that story provided an effective illustration.

Your story must make you relatable to the audience

Let's say you know the point you are making and you have selected a story that will illustrate that point. Now all you have to do is make yourself the hero of the story, right? Actually, no. This is the second big mistake speakers make when using stories. They build themselves up too much.

What happens when you build yourself up too much—when you are the hero of all your stories—is that your listeners will start to see you as someone special who has not faced the same obstacles they are facing. When you present your central premise that is supposed to be the solution to their problem or the relief from their pain, they are likely to say to themselves, "Well, of course that worked for her, but that doesn't mean it will work for me." Thus you undermine the effectiveness of your message.

The alternative is to let your audience see that you are an ordinary person who has faced the same obstacles they are facing, except that you have found (or been led to) the solution to those obstacles. This is the second key objective of your stories: making yourself relatable. You want to present yourself as someone ordinary, while presenting your solution as something special. Or, as Craig Valentine so eloquently states it, "Put the process, not the person, on the pedestal."

How do you do that? Through a variety of storytelling techniques:

1. *Make someone else the hero.* In essence, your story should not be "Look at the wonderful thing I know!" Rather, for the most effective acceptance of your idea, the story should be "Look at the problem I had (like yours) and the wonderful solution that someone revealed to me!" That someone is the hero of the story, not you. Think of that person as your guru or mentor. Make it clear that if not for the wisdom that mentor imparted to you—which you are now imparting to your audience—you would still be suffering in the same way your audience is. Then they are more likely to think, "Well,

if that worked for her, it can work for me, too!"
2. *Put the best lines in someone else's mouth.* This is closely related to the previous technique. In later chapters, you will learn the importance of using quoted dialogue in your stories. For now, just understand that when you give yourself all the best lines, you are putting yourself on a pedestal again. Shine the spotlight on the other characters in your story. Whether someone else is the hero or a supporting character, give that person the lines that reveal and support the wisdom behind your premise. Sharing the spotlight is a great way to take some of the focus off yourself so it can fall instead on the solution you are offering.
3. *Tell of your failures and flaws.* We all like to tell of our successes. But if we want our listeners to relate to us, we need to tell about our not-so-great moments. That's why I tell about falling on my face. It's also why I tell about the embarrassing moment in a Reno hotel parking lot when I totally lost face in front of the project team I was supposed to be leading. When I start a two-day project management seminar with that story, people can relate. They know I'm not putting myself on a pedestal. What

are some moments you can share that will show your audience you started out where they are now, or where they have been?

For a real connection, engage on multiple levels

Make a point, and make you relatable to your audience. These are two specific objectives you will want to keep in mind as you select and craft your story. And, as you learned in Chapter One, stories are the key to forming an emotional connection with the audience. The third specific objective, therefore, is to *engage* the listener. I define engagement as creating the space where an emotional connection can form. When a listener feels engaged with your message, he will feel you are speaking directly to him and his needs.

Your goal should be to engage your listeners on several levels at once. This is how you overcome the challenge of having different personality styles and learning styles represented in your audience. Analytical thinkers, for example, will apply their critical thinking skills to your evidence—but, whether they know it or not, they will still make an emotional decision whether to accept it. Relaters won't care as much about your evidence as about how relatable you are. Regardless of their style, you can still reach them all by using stories to engage on multiple levels.

Here are some techniques for doing that:

Engage the senses. Imagine your story in your own mind. What are you (or, if not you, what is your central character) seeing, hearing, smelling, and feeling? Use this information to place your listener in the scene.

> *One June day about twenty years ago, I found myself hiking up a mountain near Breckenridge, Colorado, with a client, to look at a communications site located at 12,000 feet elevation. We were walking because I, in my hubris (being new to the mountains), had thought I could drive us up, until we were stopped by a snowbank across the road.*

That setup doesn't really engage your senses, does it? But let me continue:

> *We were already over 11,000 feet up when we started hiking. I had only moved to Colorado the year before, after living close to sea level. To say I quickly got winded was an understatement! With each step, the air got thinner. Pretty soon, it was take two steps <huff> and pause for a breath <puff>. It was too discouraging to look up at how far was left to go, so I remember looking at my feet and noticing tiny yellow and purple flowers in the springy tundra. We were above the timberline, but I could still catch the scent of evergreens wafting up on the breeze from the valley below.*

How many ways were your senses engaged by that description? Notice how the description was woven right into the narration. It wasn't simply presented as a list: "I saw this, I smelled this, I felt this." As you will see in Chapter Five, some ways of presenting descriptions engage the listener more than others. For now, I will leave you with this thought: if you don't see it yourself, your audience won't see it, either.

Create and sustain tension. Remember what Paul Zak said about boosting oxytocin levels? To sustain attention, a story must develop tension during the narrative. That means there must be some sort of conflict. If you find "conflict" too strong a word, then substitute "striving." Someone in the story is striving for something, and is prevented, initially, from getting it.

Your high school literature teacher probably taught you that every story contains one of three types of conflict: man versus man, man versus nature, or man versus himself. At least that's the way I remember hearing it. Nowadays I might use more gender-inclusive language, but you get the idea. I find that "man-vs.-man" conflicts are rare in my stories. Most of my personal stories are about my internal struggles. The best way to show an internal struggle is to reveal it through internal dialogue. Continuing my earlier story...

> There I was, out of breath, trying not to lose face with Dan, my client, who lived in Breckenridge at 10,000 feet and was not even breathing hard as he waited patiently for me to make my way up the mountain. I said to myself, "David, this is all your fault. You could have listened to your boss, who said that road wouldn't be clear till July, but no—you

knew better. And now here you are, wasting your client's time and embarrassing yourself when all you wanted to do was show how competent you are!" As we climbed higher, my spirits sank lower, as I beat myself up mentally for getting into this situation.

Even in a story this simple, there is room (and a need) for conflict or tension. Otherwise it's just a story about going for a walk. Similarly, when I tell the story of being a circus clown for a day, the story begins with me outside the circus tent, saying to myself, "Get in, get out, don't make a fool of yourself!" This is how I reveal my internal struggle to avoid embarrassment at all cost. (Don't judge me—I was twenty years old!)

Once you have set up a conflict, to make the story even more engaging, escalate the conflict before resolving it. You will learn more about this in the next chapter as we look at story models. For now, just remember that tension sustains attention.

What is the central tension, striving, or conflict in your story? How is it revealed to the audience? How can you escalate it before resolving it? These are questions that will guide you as you seek to create engagement through your story.

Show the audience the change you want them to make. Once you have set up the tension and gotten the oxytocin flowing, remember that the greater the tension, the more empathy the audience will feel toward your central character (or protagonist). The greater the empathy, the more they will want the change your protagonist experiences. Take advantage of that empathy by modeling the desirable change you want your listeners to make.

> *My confidence in my competence was in tatters as I stumbled up the mountain toward the communication site. Then Dan, who was a few yards ahead of me, stopped and said something to me I'll never forget. He said, "Can you believe somebody is paying us to do this?" I stopped, raised my head, and looked around at what he was seeing. Coming into view over the ridge were the 14,000-foot peaks of the Continental Divide. Down on the valley floor was the town of Breckenridge, and beyond that, a view of the Mount of the Holy Cross. It was the perfect time of year to see the famous white cross formation emerging as the snow melted off that mountain. I was surrounded by breathtaking beauty. And all I could think was, "I screwed up. I'm not demonstrating my competence to be in charge here." It took Dan giving me a different perspective on the situation for me to realize that my point of view needed to shift. My spirits rose as I shook off the burden of all the invisible critics I was carrying with me. They didn't deserve to go up that mountain.*

If you can't change the situation you're in, a change in perspective is sometimes all you need. That's the change

I want my listeners to make in their thinking. Recall your specific purpose: you are speaking to make a difference. What, precisely, is the difference you want to make, and how can you model it through story?

So there you have it. Every story you use in a speech should strive to accomplish three objectives: make a point, make you relatable to your audience, and create engagement at multiple levels. In the next several chapters, you will pick up the actual recipes for forming stories that accomplish these objectives.

But first, a word is in order. Rather, there are two words we need to consider: "facts" and "truth." I am sometimes asked, "How much leeway do I have to stray from the facts in telling a story?" There are several factors to consider in answering this.

The first is that I recommend against ever telling someone else's story and representing it as your own. That's not to say that every story you tell must be something you experienced yourself (though the best stories often will be). Just don't borrow someone else's story and plug yourself into it as if it happened to you. You will never be able to tell it with authenticity that way. If you must use someone else's story, tell how it relates to you personally. The audience wants to know that the story is meaningful to you and that you didn't simply lift it from *Chicken Soup for the Soul*. "The first time I heard this story, it really opened my eyes to something I'd been struggling with" is one way to do that.

But the more challenging aspect to answering the facts-vs.-fiction question is to say just how factual a story needs to be in its retelling. Here, I like the advice of Darren LaCroix, who says what's most important is the emotional truth of the story. When you are telling a personal story, you are telling a memory, not showing a video of what happened. Given the malleability of memory over time, I don't think anyone expects your story to match up exactly with what such a hypothetical video might show. This is why I say things like, "Put the best lines in someone else's mouth," instead of making certain you are precisely documenting each person's dialogue.

In short, making a point that is *true* is more important than presenting documentary *facts* in the form of a story. (Please note, this is only your stories I am talking about. Fabricating evidence that is represented as factual is another thing entirely.)

As writer Doris Lessing put it, "There is no doubt fiction makes a better job of the truth." I'm not saying your personal stories should be fictitious. But there is nothing wrong with taking a little literary license in recounting actual events. Just don't ever hold out someone else's story as your own.

CHAPTER 3

Know your tools: what elements are needed

> "You can fix anything but a blank page."
>
> **NORA ROBERTS**

Now that you understand the importance of using stories to connect with your audience, as well as the specific objectives a story should accomplish, you are ready to start creating. In this chapter, you will pick up models you can use as checklists to ensure your stories contain the needed elements. I would say you will pick up three separate models, but two of them are closely related, so let's call it two and a half.

For discussion purposes, I will assume that you are working to create a story from some event in your own life.

However, these models are equally applicable if you are relating events that happened to other people.

Start with tension: the A-B-C Model

Recall what has been said in the previous chapters about the importance of creating tension, or conflict, within your story. Without tension or conflict, there is no story, but rather (at best) a mildly amusing anecdote. We want a story that creates and then resolves some tension, so that the listener's oxytocin production is stimulated, which in turn creates empathy for your protagonist (central character). In the best stories, the conflict is not set up and then simply resolved. Instead, the storyteller ratchets up the tension by escalating the conflict before it is resolved.

What we want, therefore, is a tool for ensuring that we set up that tension or conflict from the very start. The simplest model I know for helping to do that is one I learned years ago from master trainer Ed Tate. It is the "A-B-C Model" of storytelling. It can be described in one sentence: "**A** wants **B** despite **C**."

What this means is that "**A**" is the central character, or protagonist, of the story. That protagonist wants something, represented by "**B**." The object of desire may be a person (Prince Charming), a thing (the One Ring), or a condition (to live happily ever after). Whatever **B** is, **A** must want it above all else, and that desire is what sets the story in motion. But there is an obstacle, and that is "**C**." Something stands in the way of **A** attaining **B**. Otherwise, there would be no story. The need to overcome the obstacle sets up the conflict.

You can apply this model to any story you know. Cinderella wants to meet the prince despite her evil stepsisters. The Three Little Pigs want a safe place to live despite the Big, Bad Wolf (and poor building techniques). Dorothy wants to go home from Oz despite a number of obstacles, including a wicked witch who wants her shoes and a wizard with no magical powers. **A** wants **B** despite **C**.

Remember the story from Chapter Two about me trudging up the mountain? Clearly, I was **A**. What did I want? To appear competent and in control. Despite what? The physical challenge of the elevation gain, and the mental challenge of beating myself up over it.

Now apply that model to the story you want to construct. What does the protagonist want, and what is the obstacle? All too often, people treat a story as simply introducing a character or situation and then relating events as they happened. This approach will not sustain your listeners' interest and attention. Instead, look for the desire and the obstacle to achieving that desire. This is where you will find your conflict—the tension that sustains attention.

Build your story on a sound skeleton

You may have already noticed where the A-B-C Model comes up short. While it is a great tool for helping you to focus quickly on the central tension or conflict, it does not tell you where to go next. For that, we need a model with more moving parts. One such model is the five-part "Skeletal Story," which was created by Craig Valentine. Here are the five parts:

1. Character
2. Conflict
3. Cure
4. Change
5. Carry-out message

To relate this to the A-B-C Model, note that **A** is the central *character* (there will likely be other characters as well). **B**, the desire, and **C**, the obstacle to that desire, set up the *conflict*. Where this new model takes us further is in steps three through five, the *cure*, *change*, and *carry-out message*. These elements complete what is often called the "story arc."

Let's look at each one individually.

The *cure* is the point in the story where the obstacle (or final obstacle, if more than one) is removed. Another word for *cure* might be *climax*, as it is the point of highest tension.

The *change* is what happens to the central character after the tension is resolved. Let's assume that character is you. How were you changed by the experience? How is your world, or your outlook on the world, different?

The *carry-out message* can also be thought of as the moral of the story. To make your story memorable, try to come up with a short, catchy carry-out message.

There are other elements we have not mentioned yet. For example, you may be wondering where dialogue and vivid descriptions come into play. We will look at those later as we move to yet another model with more elements to it. The key point to understand about the Skeletal Story model is that until these five elements are in place, there is no need to add things like dialogue and description, because the story will not carry their weight, so to speak. You must have the bare bones before you can put on the flesh.

An excellent exercise is to tell your story in only five sentences, using one sentence for each element. Here is what my mountaintop story might sound like:

> *I was hiking up to a mountaintop communications site with Dan, my client, who was more accustomed to the elevation than I was. It was me against the mountain, and the mountain almost won. Finally, Dan said something that changed my perspective. Afterward, though I was still out of breath, I could stop berating myself and appreciate the beauty of the situation. Sometimes all it takes is a change in perspective.*

Clearly, this is a stripped-down version of the story. Why tell it that way? Because it forces you to concentrate on the essentials. Unless those five elements are present and clear in your own mind, the story will not have value for your audience.

Which of the five elements do you think is most important? While they are all important, one is most often overlooked by speakers: the *change*. Next time you hear a speaker tell a story, notice whether he or she ends the story right at the climax. You will likely find, as I have, that this is a common mistake.

When you fail to take your audience through the change, you miss the opportunity to make your audience desire that change for themselves, which is the whole point of telling a story. To be sure you are not guilty of that mistake, use the Skeletal Story model and tell your story in five sentences before you develop it further. Be sure all five are completely clear in your own mind before proceeding. If you don't have a change, you don't have a story that will make a difference.

Create more engagement with the Nine C's

Once you know your story has enough basic elements to stand on its own, you can start fleshing it out in ways that will truly draw your listeners in and have them on the edge of their seats. Craig Valentine is an expert at this. Did you notice how the elements of his Skeletal Story model all start with the letter "C"? In fact, they are a subset of what Craig calls his "9 C's of Storytelling." I believe he developed the 9 C's first, and then noticed that a subset of those elements had to be present before the story was worth embellishing with the remaining four elements. Therefore, the Skeletal Story model can be thought of as the smaller sibling of the full-blown "9 C's." That is why I say you are getting 2 ½ story models.

Here, then, are the 9 C's:

1. Curiosity
2. Circumstance
3. Character
4. Conflict

5. Cure
6. Change
7. Carry-out message
8. Call-backs
9. Conversations in dialogue

Did you notice the five in the middle? You are already familiar with those. Let's look at the others.

Curiosity is what draws the listeners in and makes them want to hear the story in the first place. A good way to capture their curiosity is to ask a question that hints at the point to be made by the story, without giving it away. Here are some examples:

- Have you ever found yourself in a situation where people are looking at you and you don't have a clue what you are supposed to do?
- What do you suppose is the number-one thing that stands between people and their dreams?
- How often have you let your inner critic get the better of you?

When you tease your audience with questions like these, you are laying the groundwork for them to be curious about what comes next. That makes them all the more receptive to your story.

Circumstance refers to the initial situation that the

protagonist is in. I was hiking up a mountain because snow had blocked the road. Or I was waiting outside a circus tent because my boss at the radio station said, "Go be the clown." One key to effective storytelling is to tell just enough about the circumstances to let the listener's imagination fill in the rest, without over-telling it. A common mistake is to weigh a narrative down with too much backstory. We will come back to this in the next chapter.

Call-backs are statements that refer to a previous story element or point in your speech. If you used a question to capture the audience's curiosity before you set up the story (this is called a "tease"), then a call-back could be where you reference that tease again at the end of the story, to bring it full circle and emphasize the point. For example, let's say I had set up the mountaintop story by asking the third question above about your inner critic. When I then say, "The going got a lot easier then because I left behind my inner critic, who did not deserve to be carried up the mountain on my back," that's a call-back.

Conversations in dialogue are a very powerful (and often under-used) tool for putting your audience in the scene. You want your audience to hear actual dialogue between characters, not simply a narration that implies dialogue has taken place. "She told me to stop what I was doing" is not nearly as powerful as, "She yelled, 'Stop that! Right now!'"

Similarly, "He said he loved me" doesn't put me in the scene the way a simple "I love you!" would. To put your audience in the scene, let them hear what the characters are actually saying to each other. This not only engages your audience more deeply but also helps you to create tension—which, remember, builds empathy for your protagonist—and, when the time comes, to release that tension and get a laugh from a character's verbal reaction. We'll come back to that in Chapter Six.

One thing to keep in mind about dialogue is that it doesn't always require two characters. Internal dialogue is a powerful tool for revealing internal conflict. You probably remember that from Chapter Two, where you learned about the different types of conflict.

To bring dialogue to life requires attention to some specific delivery techniques, which you will pick up in Chapter Five. For now, just remember that conversations in dialogue are an essential element of the 9 C's.

You may have noticed that I have not said much to this point about using descriptive language as a story element. That is because I prefer to treat description as part of the assembly process for your story, which is the subject of the next chapter.

Now that you have three (or 2 ½) story models to choose from, you may be wondering how to proceed. Is there one model you should choose above the others? Do you use one exclusively or somehow combine them? What I recommend is that you use all three in the sequence I presented them. The A-B-C Model will help you think of what strong desire propels the protagonist to action. Once you know that, add the turning points in the story until you can tell it in five sentences using the Skeletal Story model. I strongly urge you to complete this step before adding any more of the 9 C's. Be very clear on the change, especially, so you don't make the mistake of ending at the cure. The following questions may help guide you through the process:

- Who is the central character?
- What is that character's situation (circumstance) at the start?
- What does he or she want above all else?
- What are the obstacles to satisfying that desire?
- How and by whom are those obstacles removed?
- How are the characters changed by what happens?
- What did characters say that helped reveal the answers to these questions?
- What can you ask the audience to pique their curiosity before you start?

When you have your answers, then you may proceed to Chapter Four and start putting it all together.

CHAPTER 4

Assemble your winning story

"The more you leave out, the more you highlight what you leave in."
HENRY GREEN

Your purpose is clear in your mind, as are all the story elements described in Chapter Three. You are ready to assemble those elements into a story that will illustrate your point, make you real to your audience, and engage them on multiple levels. Sounds like a tall order, doesn't it? You may be relieved to know that you have already done the heavy lifting by answering the questions at the end of the previous chapter. What remains now is to overcome three challenges most speakers face when trying to craft a story: not loading it down, finding the right amount of description, and telling it conversationally.

Challenge #1: Overloading the story

Once, at a Toastmasters conference, I heard a speaker in the Humorous Speech Competition recount an amusing incident that took place at a roadside playground. I must admit, the central image of a grown woman struggling with a child-sized piece of playground equipment made me laugh. My overall enjoyment of the speech, however, was marred by the amount of time the speaker spent on backstory. The humor of the situation did not depend in the least on why the two women were traveling that particular highway and not some other one, thanks to someone else's change of plans. Ever since, that seven-minute speech has stayed with me as an example of how not to spend that crucial time at the start of a speech. I wonder how much funnier it could have been if the speaker had pared the story to its essentials and spent more time on the funny bits.

That is the challenge most speakers face. They burden a story with too much irrelevant information. We never knew what happened to Dorothy Gale's parents, or why she was living with Aunt Em and Uncle Henry before the tornado whisked her off to Oz, and we didn't need to know. A well-told story will give us just enough information to understand the protagonist's circumstances and to make her sympathetic. Any more than that detracts from the pursuit of her heart's desire, which should be your focus.

When assembling your story, therefore, spend some time stripping it down to its essentials, especially in the beginning. What is the absolute minimum we need to know about why you were there, in that time and place, facing that particular challenge? Especially in the case of a first-person story, you will know far more about the situation than we, the listeners, need to know. If in doubt, do a trial run. Strip the story down further than you think necessary, and then tell it to a friend who isn't familiar with it. If that person seems confused by something, perhaps you need to put in a little more information. But until you reach that point, there is a good chance you are putting in too much, not too little.

Challenge #2: Finding the right amount of description

In the case of the first challenge, the rule "less is more" will usually help you. Not so with the second challenge, which is how much description to include. This requires more of a "Goldilocks" approach: finding the "just right" amount—not too much, and not too little.

The key here is that you want to engage your listeners' imaginations. To do that, include just enough information to start painting the picture, and then leave the rest for their imaginations to fill in. That prompts two questions: How much description is just right? And is it different in speaking than in writing?

The second one is easier to answer: yes. There is a difference between the best amounts of description in a story you tell compared with a story you write down. This is one of several distinctions one can make between written and spoken language, along with vocabulary and sentence structure. Of course, even in print, many writers overdo description. Perhaps Herman Melville can get away with pages of description about how whale fat is rendered, but most writers can't. Even so, when a story is written down, the reader has the choice of how to engage with descriptive passages—whether to linger indulgently or skim them—a choice which, of course, the listener to your story does not have.

As a speaker, therefore, you have an obligation to provide the "just right" amount of description in your stories. Use too little, and you will miss the opportunity to draw the listener into the world of your story:

> *From out of nowhere, a woman walked up to me...*

Too much, and your listeners will start over-processing, where they lag behind your narrative as they mentally try to fit all the pieces of description together. Then they are likely to miss what you say next, which is most likely the action at the heart of your story:

> *As I savored the sweet, nutty aroma of my Pike's Place brew, a statuesque woman with dark hair to match her eyes approached me wearing a blue, floral-print frock with a hint of green...*

When the amount of description is just right, the listeners quickly get just enough information to draw them into the scene, while leaving them free to fill in details in their own imaginations:

Just as I could start to smell the coffee brewing, a tall brunette in a blue dress walked up to me...

Did you see what I did there? I began the same scene three ways. The first one contained nothing memorable, while the second one is (I hope you will agree) amateurishly over-written. The last one grabs your attention while leaving your imagination free to fill in the details of the woman in blue. Notice, too, how it draws on two senses: smell and sight. It's always a good idea to involve more than one sense in your descriptions, as long as you don't over-write as in example number two.

In one of my workshops, I tell a story about a 98-year-old woman named Gertrude who, when I knew her, still lived alone and had her son drive her to church nearly every Sunday. The story includes this line: "Every Sunday, her son John would pull right up to her front door in his black, F-150 pickup and help her into it." Hours later, I can ask the participants who remembers what John drove, and someone will always answer, "A black F-150." (Where I live, everyone knows an F-150 is the most common Ford pickup.) This drives home a related point, that including a color or a number is often the easiest way to add just enough detail to a story to make it memorable (hence the blue dress). The two points work together: engage the senses with just enough detail to bring a scene to life and make it memorable, while giving the listeners plenty of room to fill in more details in their own minds. That's how you find the Goldilocks spot and make your descriptions "just right."

Challenge #3: Using conversational language

The third challenge also relates to the difference between written and spoken language. So let's consider what some of those differences are. Unlike someone reading an unfamiliar word, a listener does not have the luxury of putting a book down and grabbing a dictionary (or, more likely, a smartphone). Similarly, your listener is unlikely to interrupt you and ask you to go back when you lose him in a complex, convoluted sentence. So when we speak, we need to use shorter, simpler sentences and familiar words.

Telling a story is no time to show off your vocabulary. How likely are you to use "gazed" in conversation? Then when you say, "I gazed out the window" instead of "I glanced" or "I looked," you are calling attention to yourself, which gets in the way of building engagement with your audience. Only use words you would use if you were relating your story to me in conversation over a cup of coffee.

The reason this is a challenge for most speakers is because they are not accustomed to writing in their speaking voice. This is an acquired skill that takes a good bit of practice. But fear not, because there is an easy work-around: simply tell your story to someone, record yourself telling it, and transcribe that recording.

After many years of speaking, I still use this technique often. I use a pocket-sized, digital voice recorder, but chances are you can find the same functionality on your smartphone. Just be sure to give your listener permission to raise an eyebrow or otherwise signal you when they hear you use a pretentious word or a wordy sentence construction where a simpler one will do.

Use the techniques in this chapter to overcome the three biggest challenges most speakers face when constructing a story. Then move on to Chapter Five to learn how to fine-tune the telling of the story.

CHAPTER 5

You had to be there: how to tell it

"A story has its purpose and its path. It must be told correctly for it to be understood."

MARCUS SEDGWICK

Up to now, everything you have been asked to do, except for talking your story into a recording device in Chapter Four, could be done with your mouth closed. Whether you realized it or not, it has all been about *writing* your story. I do encourage you to write it down, rather than trying to keep it in your head. Only when a story is written down can it be examined to be sure the needed elements are all there, and edited for clarity and brevity.

But starting with this chapter, you have to get on your

feet and start speaking. That is the only way you can hope to master some of the subtle techniques that make your story come alive.

Take us; don't tell us

Remember, the main reason you, as a speaker, are telling a story is to build connection with your audience. Anything you do that says, "This is a story; watch me tell it!" will take the listener out of the story and break that connection. That means you don't want to call attention to your delivery techniques. You want to keep them subtle, almost unnoticed. Still, you need to be aware of them. Storytelling techniques, properly employed, will set you apart from other speakers in ways your audience may not even be able to name.

The techniques in this chapter are best summed up by this statement: "Take us; don't tell us." When you are relating a story, it is not enough to have constructed it using pretty words. If you want to move your audience, you must *relive* the events you are telling about. Every time I tell the story of hiking up that mountain, I have to bring to mind the physical and emotional sensations I was experiencing—the effort, the shortness of breath, the feeling of inadequacy. If I fail to do that, the story will not resonate. It will be just so many words.

To take us into your story, use the following techniques:

1. Go into the scene yourself, in your own mind. Your description of a scene will come across differently if you are describing

what you *saw*, for example, compared with seeing it in your mind's eye and describing what you *are seeing*. The latter is more likely to ring true in the audience's ears.
2. Describe your emotional state as directly as possible. I hear speakers say things like "You can imagine how devastated I felt," when a simple "I was devastated," accompanied by appropriate facial expression and body language, conveys the idea more powerfully.
3. Pause long enough for the audience to imagine what you are describing. If you are seeing it (or hearing it, etc.) yourself, you are more likely to do this. I have seen many speakers ruin otherwise good description by rushing through it. This is especially important when you are engaging different senses, as your listeners have to switch their attention accordingly.
4. Limit gestures to ones you would use in a conversation. If you move about in an exaggerated way, miming every aspect of what you are narrating, you will call attention to yourself and take us out of the story. On the other hand, if you are truly reliving what happened to you, your movements will likely be more spontaneous and therefore authentic.

5. Use the stage appropriately. Don't distract us with random movement or pacing back and forth. If your story takes place in several locations, place those locations clearly on the stage in your mind's eye, just a couple of steps apart, and move between those specific locations at appropriate times in the story. Or, if your story takes place over time, create a timeline on the stage using a location for each time period. The timeline should progress from the audience's left to right, so when you tell of the earliest events, place yourself as far to your right as possible.
6. Speaking of time, *when* an event takes place is the first thing your listeners want to hear, so that they can properly organize what follows in a mental framework. For example, take the statement "I was walking to church last Sunday when I saw a bright red convertible come speeding around the corner." The two actions you described—walking and seeing—are separated by the time reference. That causes just a moment of mental confusion while the listener's brain sorts the information into the proper order. In the meantime, they have missed a few words, which in this case might be the important description of the car. Instead,

lead the listener through the scene by placing the information in a more logical order, starting with the time reference: "Last Sunday, I was walking to church when I saw a bright red convertible come speeding around the corner." The distinction may seem trivial, but it will make a difference in your listener's comprehension.

Beware the dialogue trap

You will recall from Chapter Three that one of the essential 9 C's of storytelling is conversations in dialogue. As with description, however, there is a "sweet spot" you must find between too much and too little dialogue in comparison with the narration. Too little, and you miss the chance to draw the listener into the scene and to reveal your character's thoughts and reactions. Too much, however, and you risk losing us again as we wait impatiently for the action to advance. In general, you don't want the characters in your story to exchange more than about three lines each before you break the pattern with narration.

    A second pitfall to watch out for with dialogue is the overuse of the verb "said" and its synonyms. Instead of "I said…she said…I said…" simply let us see who is talking by your delivery technique. Here is how to do that:

1. Don't make eye contact with your audience when relating dialogue. The character in your story was not talking to the audience.

2. Instead, use the technique of "locus and focus" (for which I am grateful to my high school oral-interpretation teacher). That means you mentally *locate* each character in a specific place with the respect to the other character (this works best if there are only two), and you *focus* your gaze on where the other character should be when you speak. Put one character slightly to the left of centerline and the other character slightly to the right.
3. Don't overdo it. Your gaze need not shift more than about thirty degrees to make the distinction between characters clear. Some speakers make the mistake of swiveling from one full-profile view to the other. This is distracting.
4. Don't move your feet when changing characters. You will see speakers sometimes step back and forth between the two characters' supposed locations in space. This is cartoonish, unnecessary, and distracting. The shift of gaze from left to right is all we need.
5. If there is a significant height difference between the two characters, let us see that by shifting your gaze *slightly* up and down as you shift from left to right. Again, don't overdo it.

Why does this technique work? Because we have been trained by movies and television to interpret conversation in this way. Next time you watch a scene involving dialogue between two characters, pay special attention to the way the shots of the actors are intercut. You will almost always see one character looking slightly to the right of the camera and the other character looking slightly to the left. The technique I have just described imitates this aesthetic, and that is why it works.

One final note about dialogue: be especially restrained in your use of other words for "said." You don't need to say "she replied" if I can see you replying. Similarly, instead of "he exclaimed," simply let us see and hear you exclaim! Proper delivery of dialogue is as much an acting technique as it is a speaking technique. Take us—don't tell us!

Each of these techniques in this chapter, taken on its own, may seem to make only a tiny difference. But those differences add up to a richer listening experience for your audience. Master these techniques and you, too, will have audience members coming up to you afterward saying, "I was there!"

CHAPTER 6

How to maximize your impact with humor

"A good story should make you laugh, and a moment later break your heart."

CHUCK PALAHNIUK, *Stranger than Fiction*

Congratulations. You now have the tools necessary to make a well-constructed, well-delivered story an effective part of your speech, and you have a good understanding of why it is important that you do so. Armed with these tools and this understanding, you will be able to connect with audiences in ways you may never have experienced before, and to reap the benefits of doing so. And yet, you still may wonder, "How do I make them laugh?" This chapter, while not intended to make a stand-up comedian out of you, offers some answers to this question, along with the related one: do you even *want* to make them laugh?

Why use humor at all?

As you are aware by now, I have learned the craft of storytelling from many excellent speakers, including former World Champions like Ed Tate. I take comfort from Ed's claim that of all the story elements, humor is the optional one. That's not to say Ed never gets laughs—he does. But two of the speeches Ed used to win the 2000 World Championship of Public Speaking were serious, dramatic, and heavy-hitting in their overall tone. A serious speech, in the right hands, can be a powerful tool.

And if you look back over Craig Valentine's "9 C's of Storytelling" in Chapter Three, you will notice that humor is not listed as one his essential elements, either—even though Craig is one of the funniest speakers I know.

We can conclude, therefore, that you need not get laughs to make a story effective.

There is a counter-argument to be made, however, and it is often expressed in the professional speaker's dictum, "You don't need to make them laugh—unless you want to get paid!" It is generally true that funny speakers get booked more often and command higher fees. So, yes, the use of humor as another speaking tool is something you want to consider. Just understand that stories can be effective without it.

There are two reasons why I believe humor is desirable in speaking. The first is that laughter is a release of tension.

Remember the importance of tension, from the Chapter One discussion of oxytocin? To move your audience, you must create tension in your narrative, according to Paul Zak. And that tension has to go somewhere. If you simply build it up and don't relieve it, your audience will leave feeling somehow dissatisfied. If, instead, you build it up and then give the audience a chance to laugh at some surprising way that the tension is relieved, they will feel more satisfied with the story, and consequently with you.

The second reason is that research has shown that listeners are most receptive to new information in the moment immediately following a good laugh. This makes sense when you recall that all decision-making is ultimately emotional. A happy emotional state is more conducive to the decision to accept and act upon your message.

So, on balance, I think it is a good idea for speakers to know how to get some laughs from their stories. Fortunately, that is not hard to do once you understand some simple principles. But first, you need to understand how *not* to go about getting laughs.

How most speakers get it wrong

You've seen it countless times. A speaker gets up in front of the audience, tells a lame joke, and gets a few groans intermingled with chuckles. Or he tells a long, somewhat pointless story with a punchline you see coming a mile away, and your response is, "Really? Please get on to something that is not a waste of my time!"

What are these speakers doing wrong? They are trying to *add* humor to a speech instead of *uncovering* the humor lurking in their stories. Further, in the second example the speaker is ignoring what you have already learned in preceding chapters, such as keeping the backstory to a minimum and knowing what point your story makes. (But you won't make these mistakes any longer!)

Trying to add humor, by simply adding a joke to your speech, is likely to fail unless you are skilled at creating original jokes that relate to what the audience is experiencing. That is called situational humor, and while it can be quite effective, it is beyond the scope of this chapter. Lacking this skill, most speakers simply take jokes they have heard elsewhere—or, worse, gotten from a website—and sprinkle them into their speech. In doing so, they risk their material being perceived as unoriginal by those who have heard it before, and therefore risk some loss of credibility. ("If her jokes aren't original, how do I know her ideas are?")

If, instead, you uncover the humor that is latent in your stories, you make the audience's laughter an organic part of their response to your stories—and to you! In doing so, not only do you make yourself more relatable but you also make your stories (and therefore your points) more memorable. So let's look at how to do that.

Don't add humor—uncover it in your stories

How do you uncover the humor in a story? Start with the tension. Then show how a character in the story reacts when that tension is resolved. Remember the A-B-C Model from Chapter Three? Somebody (**A**) wants something (**B**) despite an obstacle (**C**). Remove that obstacle in a surprising way, show the character's reaction, and you've got a laugh. The reaction can belong to the central character, **A**, or to a secondary character who is observing the action. (In more elaborate narratives, this character might be considered the "comic relief" in contrast to the seriousness of the protagonist.)

For example, in my seminars I often tell the story of how I transitioned to my speaking and coaching career from my earlier career in engineering. I was hired as the subject-matter expert for a training project. Then the training expert who hired me left the company, and I had to fill both roles, only I had no formal training in training design.

> *What to do? I needed to get up to speed quickly. I needed to talk to someone who knew a lot about training and would take the time to talk to me. Finally, it hit me! I picked up the phone, and I said, "Mom?...Help!"*

Of course, I pause for a laugh after "Mom?" and I always get one. (And generally a second one after "Help!") Why? First, there's tension: how will I succeed in this new role? Then, a small amount of escalation: who possesses the expertise I need and will talk to me immediately? The obstacle was my lack of knowledge about training. And the way that obstacle was removed was surprising—no one expected me to ask my mother (a retired educator) for help.

Notice, however, that the surprising release of tension in this case gets a laugh only because the audience experiences it through the character's point of view, thanks to the use of dialogue. Imagine if I had simply narrated through it by saying, "So I realized what I needed to do was to call my mom and ask her for help." Not even a chuckle.

Now, admittedly, the level of tension in that brief story is quite low. That reinforces my point: even with relatively low tension, a character's response, when revealed in dialogue, is often enough to get a laugh. The greater the tension and the more surprising its relief, the bigger the laugh.

What about having a secondary character uncover the humor? Consider the story of how I broke my arm and dislocated my elbow while performing onstage as The Cowardly Lion in a community-theatre production of *The Wizard of Oz*. My teenage daughter, who was in the show with me, ended up accompanying me to the emergency room (only after I had finished the show, I might add!) where my dislocation was fixed. She left the room during the actual procedure and came back just as I was recovering from the fast-acting anesthesia, only to hear me, in my deeply drugged state, singing a lullaby to the head physician of the emergency department! She looked at him and said, "What can I say? He does musical theatre!" With the right "look" accompanying the line, I get a laugh I'd never get if I simply tried to describe how mortified she was.

Now you have a blueprint for uncovering the humor in a story. Set up the tension, release the tension, and reveal a character's surprising reaction to the change through dialogue.

That said, there are still a couple of things to be aware of as you mine your stories for humor. First, as any comedian will tell you, the laugh you get is inversely proportional to the length of the setup. The shorter the setup, the bigger the laugh. Of course, if you take this to an extreme you will sound less like a storyteller and more like a standup comedian, who goes for a new laugh every few seconds. Your stories still have to be long enough to accomplish the objectives in Chapter Two, while keeping the backstory to a minimum as described in Chapter Four.

This is one reason I recommend writing down your stories as you work on them. Only when something is written can it be edited—tightened up in the interest of both clarity and humor. I have heard it said that comedian Jerry Seinfeld will spend hours cutting an eight-word sentence down to five words. That's not the extreme to which you want to go as a storyteller, but it gets the point across. Shorter is better.

Second, it is important for you to know where to end a line to maximize the laugh. It is not enough to know the punchline; you must know, and end on, the punch *word*. End on the most important word, and then stop and get out of the way of the laugh. If my daughter had said, "He does musical theatre. What can I say?" it would not have been nearly as funny. The punchline works because it ends on the word "theatre."

Knowing your punch word is important to a speaker not only for getting laughs, but also for making a point memorable even when you are not going for a laugh. As Fripp says, "Last words linger." "Lend me your ears, friends, Romans, and countrymen!" simply doesn't cut it.

Now you know what a story should accomplish and why, what elements are needed, how to assemble it, how to deliver it, and how to make it funny (should you choose to do so). You are ready to go forth with confidence to give more impactful, more memorable speeches by using stories effectively. You have the basic techniques. Before you use them, however, read on for two advanced techniques. One will make your speaking even more powerful, and the other will help you out when a key story component is missing.

CHAPTER 7

Advanced techniques for storytelling power

> "There's always room for a story that can transport people to another place."
>
> **J.K. ROWLING**

The central promise of this book is that you will pick up tools that help you build a stronger audience connection than you may ever have thought possible. And why would you want to build a stronger connection with your listeners? To move them to action, of course! In this final chapter, we are going to look at a couple of advanced techniques for doing just that. The first is the Push-Pull Method using two contrasting stories. The second is offered here in response to a question I sometimes get: "How do I tell a story whose ending is not yet resolved?" For that situation, you can use the tool of the Hypothetical Cure.

The Push-Pull Method

Recall the concept of your Specific Purpose from Chapter One. As a speaker, you are out to make a difference in the way your listeners think, act, or feel. Your job is to change their condition somehow—to move them from where they are to where they could be. If that were an easy change to make, they probably would have already made it without your help. But they didn't, so it's up to you to help them overcome their inertia.

There are two ways to overcome inertia and get a motionless object moving: push it, or pull it. Think of that as an analogy to what you want to do with your audience. You want to pull them away from their old condition, and give them a push in a new direction. An ideal way to do that is to tell two contrasting stories. One shows what happens to a character who remains stuck in the old condition, and the other illustrates what can happen when a character embraces the new condition. When you draw a clear contrast between the two stories, you are using the Push-Pull Method. You are using two stories to make one point.

> *It was a hot June day at the Lubbock County Fairgrounds. I was especially hot, as I was wearing an ill-fitting, rainbow-striped jumpsuit, a wig, and full clown makeup. I was outside the "big top" of Circus Vargas, waiting with a hundred other*

> performers for the cue to enter that tent in front of two thousand Lubbockites. And I didn't have a clue what I was doing. All I could say to myself was, "Get in, get out, don't make a fool of yourself!"

Thus begins the story of my one day as a circus clown, thanks to a promotional arrangement between the circus and my employer, a Lubbock, Texas, radio station. In my few minutes under that big top, I had little choice but to follow the prompting of the two clowns accompanying me. The clever routine they led me through, completely unrehearsed by me, resulted in my quickly learning to trust them, only to see them let me fall on my face—literally. In the center ring of the circus. It was their joke, and I was their fall guy. I was there to be a clown, so I played it for laughs. But to my twenty-year-old-self, it was unnerving to be in a situation where I had no idea what was expected of me or whom to trust. My fragile ego feared public embarrassment. Not a good trait if you want to be a clown!

Fast-forward a few decades. Again, I am in front of an audience in makeup and costume. Only this time, I know what I am doing. I am performing the role of The Cowardly Lion, and the show is well-rehearsed. The only part that wasn't rehearsed was my misstep that resulted in an unscripted fall from a platform to the stage floor, a drop of three or four feet.

> Someone laughed, thinking it a great pratfall. Many in the audience realized, though, that the great cat had not landed on his feet. The Tin Man came over,

and with his back to the audience he whispered, "Are you OK?"

"No, I think my arm is broken. Let's go." And the two of us, ironically, proceeded to put the legs back on the Scarecrow.

Later, in the emergency-room visit described in Chapter Six, I would learn that I had dislocated my right elbow and broken that forearm (foreleg?) in two places. But the show must go on! I finished the performance, down to the costume change to Zeke the farmhand for the final scene, where Dorothy's adventure is revealed to be (spoiler alert!) a dream.

Two stories in which I fall down unexpectedly in front of audiences. In the first, my bruised ego was the only damage. In the second, I was seriously injured. And yet, the second was a growth experience for me. I discovered the value of staying in character no matter what happens. I had a powerful connection with my fellow performers that was completely lacking at the circus. And, perhaps most important, I came to appreciate the value of rehearsal. I got through the rest of the show on the strength of what I had rehearsed.

> *When people ask me, "Why didn't you stop the show?" I answer, "Because I didn't know how." All I knew to do was what we had rehearsed—and we had never rehearsed stopping the show! In times of great stress, you will fall back on what you have rehearsed. What are you rehearsing? Are you focused on the falling down, or on the getting up?*

Two stories drive home one point through their contrast. That's the Push-Pull method. It takes a bit more time, since there are two stories to tell, but it's a powerful tool when you are able to use it.

The Hypothetical Cure

The most powerful stories—the ones that will build the strongest connection with your audience—are those you have lived, not heard. But suppose you are living out a story that has not yet drawn to a neat conclusion. After all, life is like that! You have the A-B-C elements: a character, a strong desire, and an obstacle. But the obstacle has not yet been removed, so there appears to be no cure or change, much less a carry-out message. Can you still use this story?

The answer is yes, you can, through the technique of the Hypothetical Cure.

Consider the example of a cell biologist I know who has done groundbreaking work into the cellular underpinnings of cancer. In collaboration with other scientists, she has been able to show how a specific protein mutates (changes its shape, essentially) when it is present in pancreatic cancer. For several years, she has held out the hope that this work could lead to an early-detection test for pancreatic cancer, which kills thousands of people in the U.S. alone each year—not because it is not treatable (it is), but because it is rarely detected until it has spread to other organs.

Let's apply the A-B-C Model. My scientist friend, whom I'll call Karen, is **A**. What does she want? A screening test for pancreatic cancer. What are the obstacles? There are several, as she has explained to me. Chief among them is the fact that there is currently no way to detect the mutated protein in a relatively non-invasive way like a blood or urine test.

Now imagine Karen giving a presentation to other scientists. Her specific purpose is to persuade some of them to take up the baton and continue the research in this field, despite the fact that finding funding is increasingly difficult. What is her skeletal story? Recall the exercise from Chapter Three, where you want to tell your story using five sentences, one for each skeletal element (character, conflict, cure, change, and carry-out message). Hers might start like this:

> *My colleagues and I have identified a mutated protein that seems to be specific to cancer formation in the pancreas. [Character, along with some Circumstance] We believe this knowledge could lead us to an early-detection test for this cancer, but the obstacle is that this protein is not present in blood or urine, so there's no apparent way to screen for it. [Conflict: striving meets obstacle]*

And that is where the story appears to end, for now. To carry it forward we must engage the audience's imagination using the Hypothetical Cure technique. Essentially, we are playing "What if?" Imagine that Karen continues in this vein:

> *But imagine if one of you were able to overcome this obstacle, maybe with a more sensitive blood test*

than any we can currently envision. [Hypothetical Cure] This year in our country, 50,000 people will be diagnosed with pancreatic cancer, and 40,000 will die from it. With early detection, most of those lives could be saved. [Change] This is science that saves lives. [Carry-out message]

Yes, I realize I slipped an extra sentence in there. But you get the idea. By saying "What if..." or "Imagine if..." you can lead your audience to think about how things *could* be different if the obstacle was removed, which may be enough to move them to action. Get them to imagine being the hero of the story—and then maybe they will be!

There you have it: two advanced techniques for moving your audience and changing their condition. Remember what I said on the first page? You can use these tools (and the others throughout the book) to build a stronger audience connection than you may ever have thought possible. When you do that, you become a change agent, changing the world one presentation at a time. All because you know how to construct, deliver, and use a story to its best advantage.

EPILOGUE

Your story file

In this book, you have learned how and why to use a story effectively in your speaking. "But," you may be thinking, "where do I find these stories?" Answer: the best stories come from your own life. And the best place to go for stories, the next time you start working on a speech, is your story file.

Every speaker should have a story file. Whether you keep it in a notebook that is always with you, or in a document on your computer, you need to write down ideas as they come to you. Don't worry that they're initially incomplete—just write down enough to recall the incident to mind later. I prefer to keep my story file on my computer, for ease in searching its contents, but it's a personal choice.

Can't think of anything interesting that's happened to you? Sure you can. Start writing with one of these prompts:

- Once upon a time, I...
- I'll never forget the time I...
- People love to hear me tell about the time I...
- I wish I could forget about the time I...

A word about this last one is in order. Why try to remember a painful, forgettable incident in your life? Because that's where you find your struggle, and in it perhaps the best lesson for others. What did you have to overcome? Who helped you? How was the obstacle removed? Or, if it hasn't yet been removed (see Chapter Seven), what change can you look forward to when it is?

When you start your story file, it may not be at all clear how you will use these stories. That's OK—that insight can come later, as you gain more practice in using the storytelling models in this book. For example, years ago I wrote in my story file, "Once upon a time I...was a clown in a circus." That's all I wrote. Years would go by before I gained the key insight that made that story worth telling—that I was struggling to avoid embarrassing myself in public.

You'll know when a story is ripe for the telling when you can say, at a minimum, what you were striving for and what obstacle you had to overcome. We all have desires, and I can't imagine anyone going through life without some of those desires being thwarted by obstacles at some point. That's why I can say with complete confidence: yes, you do have a story. Now tell it!

ABOUT THE AUTHOR

Since 2011, speaker, coach, trainer, and author David P. Otey has helped thousands of people on two continents in their quest for personal and professional growth. Before that, he worked in broadcast engineering for companies in Texas, Colorado, California, Indiana, and Pennsylvania. He is a contributing author to the book *World Class Speaking in Action* (2015) as well as to the *NAB Engineering Handbook, Tenth Edition* (2007), and various periodicals. A native of Port Arthur, Texas, he currently resides in Golden, Colorado.

Contact David by email at david@davidotey.com. Follow him on twitter @AuthorDavidOtey or at Facebook/OteySpeaking.

Made in the USA
Columbia, SC
12 October 2024